DRAW EUROPE

AN EASY STEP-BY-STEP APPROACH

BY
Kristin J. Draeger

Copyright 2015 by Kristin J. Draeger

All rights reserved. No part of this book may be reproduced, stored in a retrieval system, or transmitted in any form or by any means, electronic, mechanical, photocopying, recording, or otherwise, without the prior written permission of Kristin J. Draeger.

All of the maps in this book were drawn by Kristin Draeger and are copyrighted by Kristin Draeger ©2015. The majority of the tiny buildings on the cover and interior pages were drawn by Marina Zlochin and purchased through iStockphoto ©2015.

Websites:
ArtK12.com
SeriousFunK12.com
info@artk12.com

CASPIAN SEA

URAL MOUNTAINS

CASPIAN SEA

Next, place the Caspian Sea below the mountains. It kind of looks like a big, unshelled peanut. Place it carefully. Notice how big it is, and how far it is from the Ural Mountains and from the bottom of the page.

BLACK SEA

The Black Sea is west of the Caspian Sea. It looks like, well, a blob.

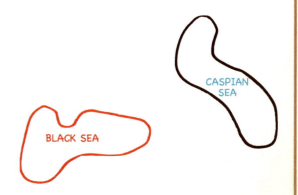

RUSSIAN BORDERS

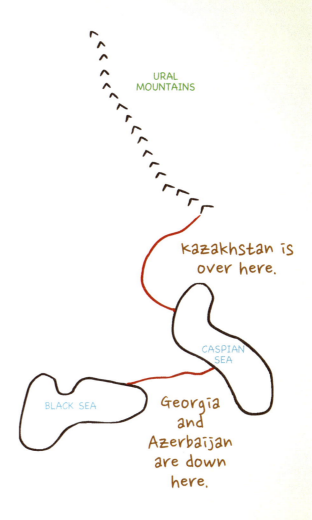

Now connect the bottom of the Ural Mountains to the Caspian Sea and then connect the Caspian Sea to the Black Sea. These are two of Russia's borders with the Middle East.

SEA OF AZOV

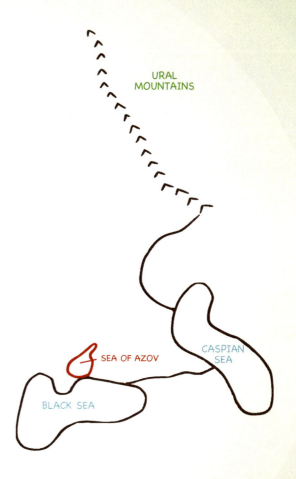

The Sea of Azov is a little body of water that sits north of the Black Sea. It looks like a drop of water falling into the Black Sea.

(WESTERN) RUSSIA

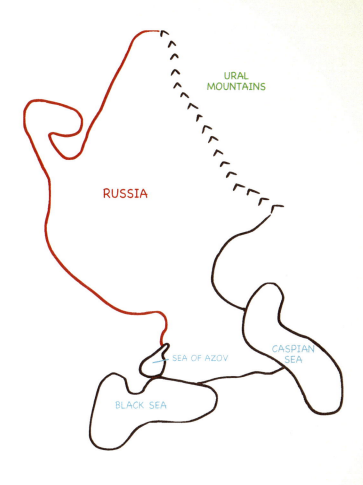

Now we will draw the western border of Russia. Remember, only the western half of Russia is considered to be part of Europe. This part of Russia looks like a dinosaur head emerging from a blob.

(WESTERN) RUSSIA

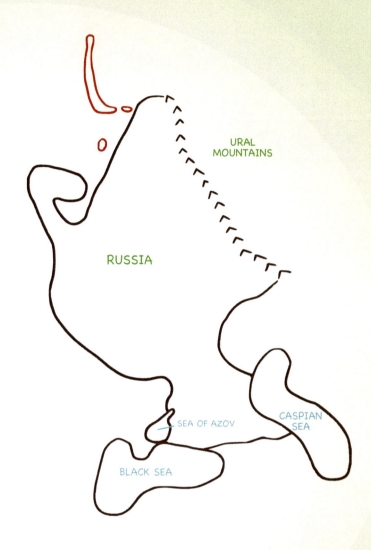

These islands are also part of Russia. The largest one, that looks like a worm crawling north, is called Novaya Zemlya.

BARENTS & KARA SEAS

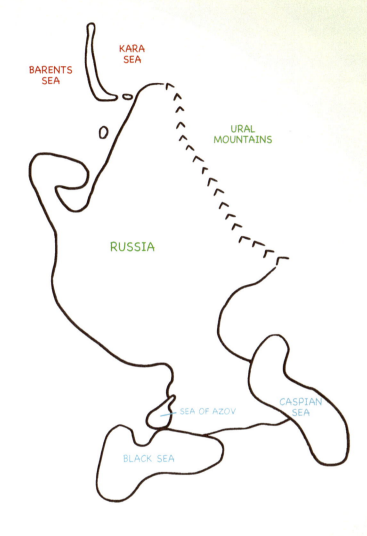

Now we are going to label two seas. The first one is the Barents Sea. This body of water is named after Dutch explorer Willem Barentsz. The second is the Kara Sea.

WHITE SEA

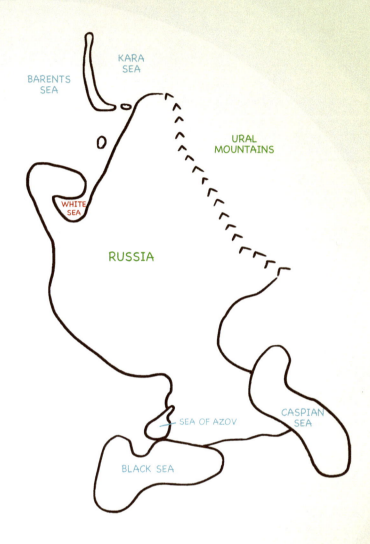

Another sea is tucked up under the dinosaur's chin. It is called the White Sea. There are four seas around the globe named after colors. Can you name them?

SANTA'S BLOB

This blob looks like Santa's bag of gifts and will contain eight countries.

SANTA'S BLOB

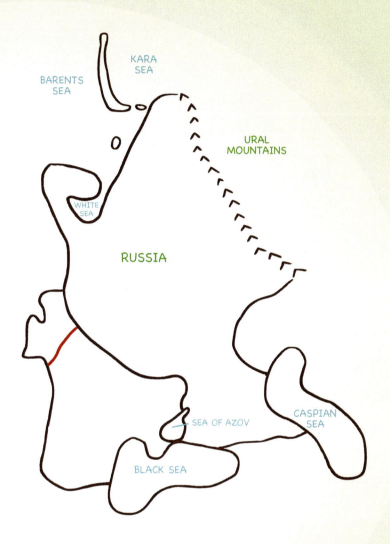

All four of the countries in the opening of Santa's bag have a shoreline on the Baltic Sea. We will label the Baltic Sea a little later.

ESTONIA

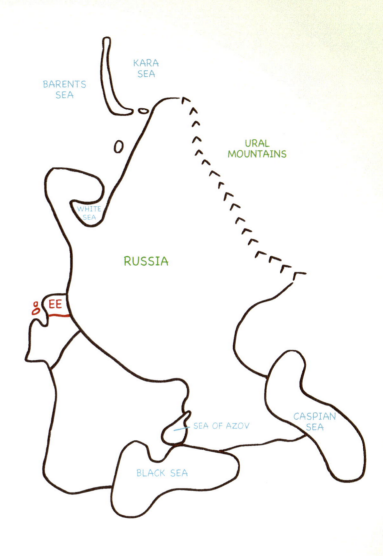

Estonia (EE) is the first country. Estonia has many islands and islets (very small islands). The two largest are drawn here. Labeling some of the smaller countries gets tricky so we are going to use the International Organization for Standardization's (ISO) two-letter codes. The ISO code for Estonia is EE.

LATVIA

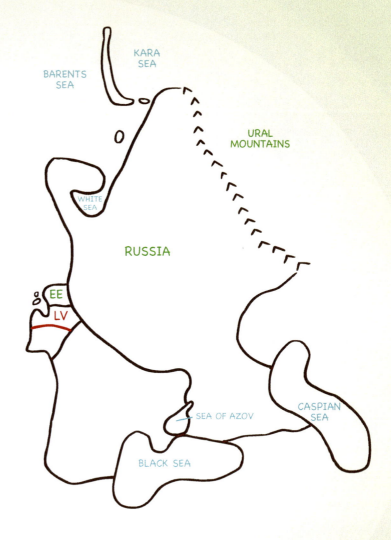

South of Estonia is the Republic of Latvia (LV).

# LITHUANIA & RUSSIA

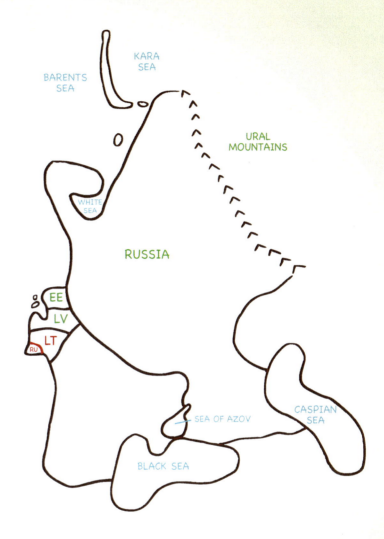

The third country in Santa's bag is the Republic of Lithuania (LT). The tiny country to the west and south of Lithuania is a detached part of Russia (RU) called Kaliningrad Oblast.

BELARUS

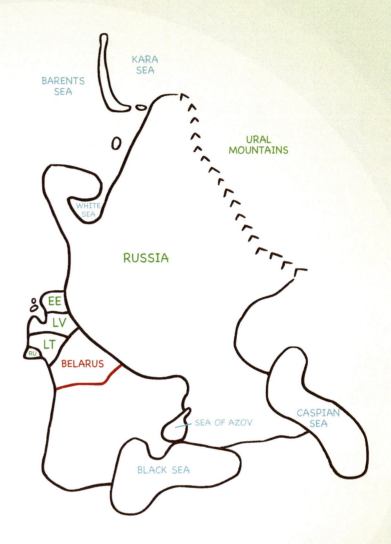

In the neck of Santa's bag is the Republic of Belarus.

UKRAINE

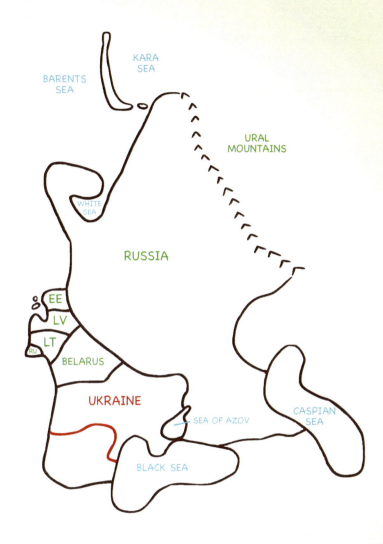

The largest country in Santa's bag is the country of Ukraine. It is the largest country that is entirely in Europe. (Obviously Russia is larger but it is not entirely in Europe.)

MOLDOVA & ROMANIA

Tucked into the side of the Ukraine is Moldova (MD), and at the bottom of Santa's bag is the country of Romania.

BALKAN BIRD BLOB

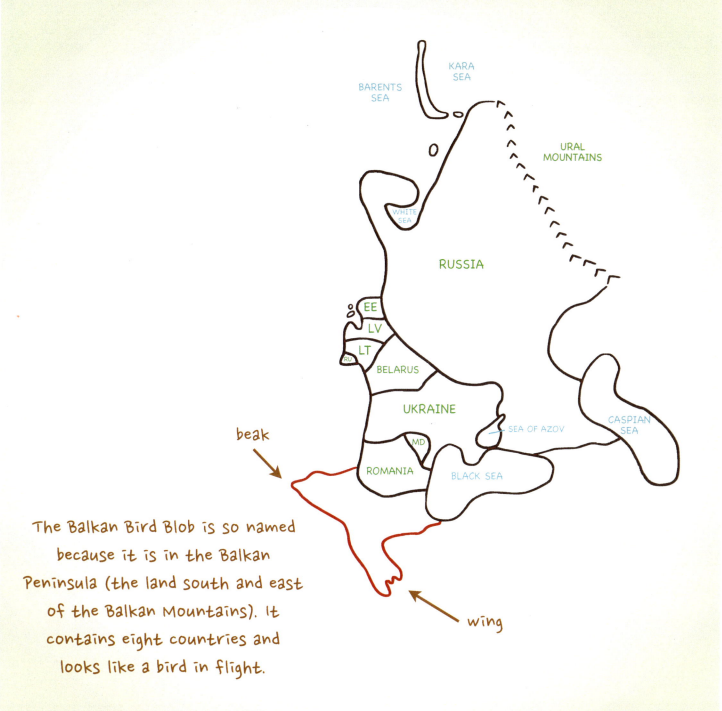

The Balkan Bird Blob is so named because it is in the Balkan Peninsula (the land south and east of the Balkan Mountains). It contains eight countries and looks like a bird in flight.

TURKEY

Turkey is a transcontinental country; this means that it has land in more than one continent. A small part of Turkey is in the continent of Europe (the solid red line) and the rest is in the continent of Asia (the dotted red line).

This is the Asian part of Turkey. Don't draw this part.

GREECE

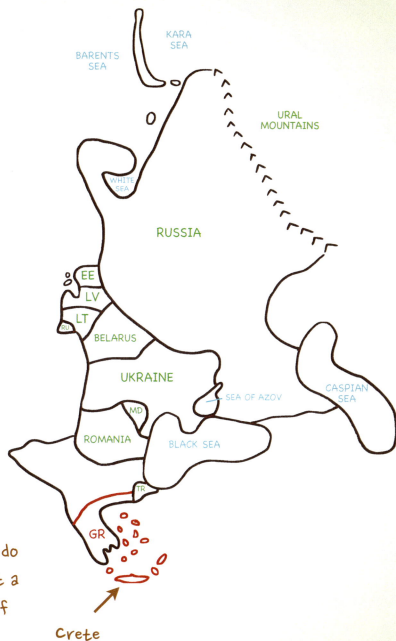

Greece (GR), the bird wing, consists of a mainland and approximately 1400 islands. You do not have to draw them all; just a few will suffice. The largest of the islands is Crete.

Crete

AEGEAN & IONIAN SEAS

Greece is surrounded by the the Aegean Sea and the Ionian Sea.

BULGARIA

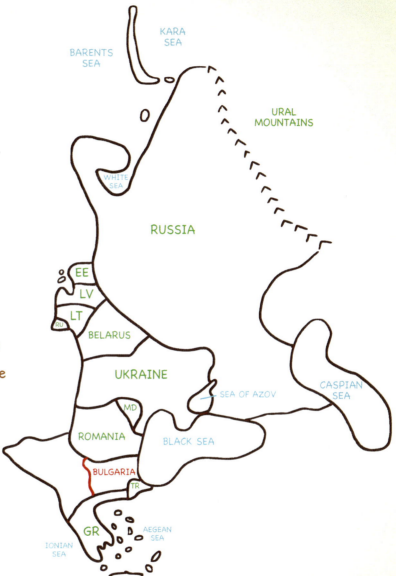

The Republic of Bulgaria is the back end of the bird, no offense to Bulgarians.

MACEDONIA

The Republic of Macedonia (MK) is in the armpit (wingpit?) of the bird. Why MK instead of MC? Good question. In the Macedonian language Macedonia is spelled "Makedonija."

SERBIA

The Republic of Serbia (RS) looks like a saddle on the back of the bird.

ALBANIA

This is the Republic of Albania (AL). It is on the bird's elbow.

MONTENEGRO

Montenegro (ME) is a very small country north of Albania.

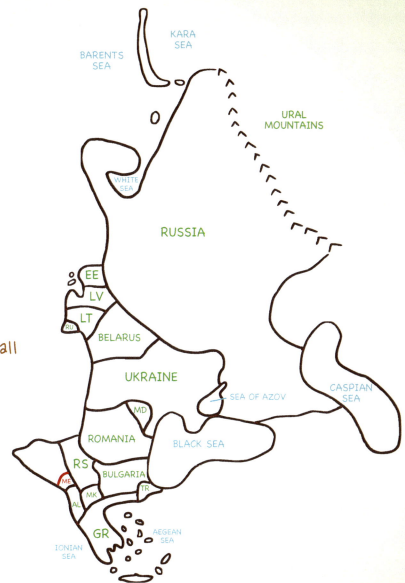

BOSNIA & HERZEGOVINA, & CROATIA

Bosnia and Herzegovina (BA) is the cheek of the bird, and Croatia (HR) is the beak of the bird. Why HR? In Croatian, Croatia is spelled "Hrvatska."

HAMSTER BLOB

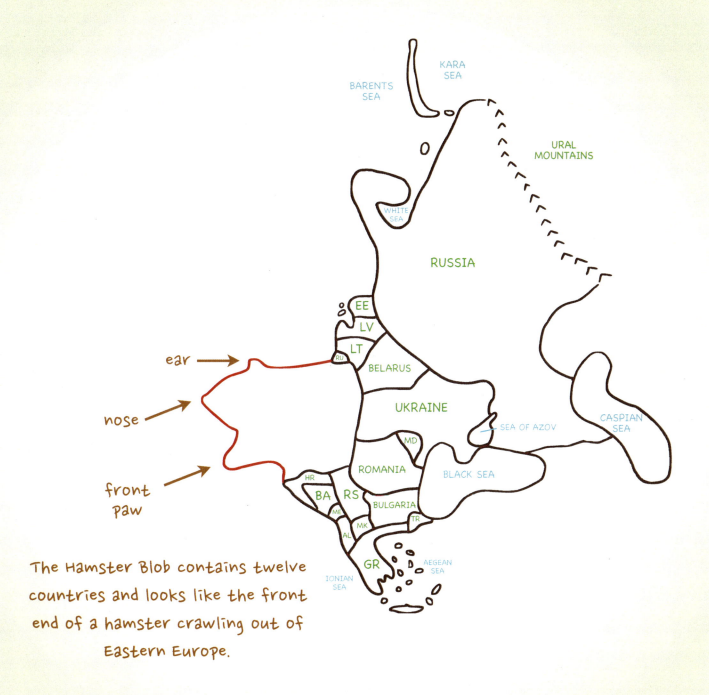

The Hamster Blob contains twelve countries and looks like the front end of a hamster crawling out of Eastern Europe.

POLAND

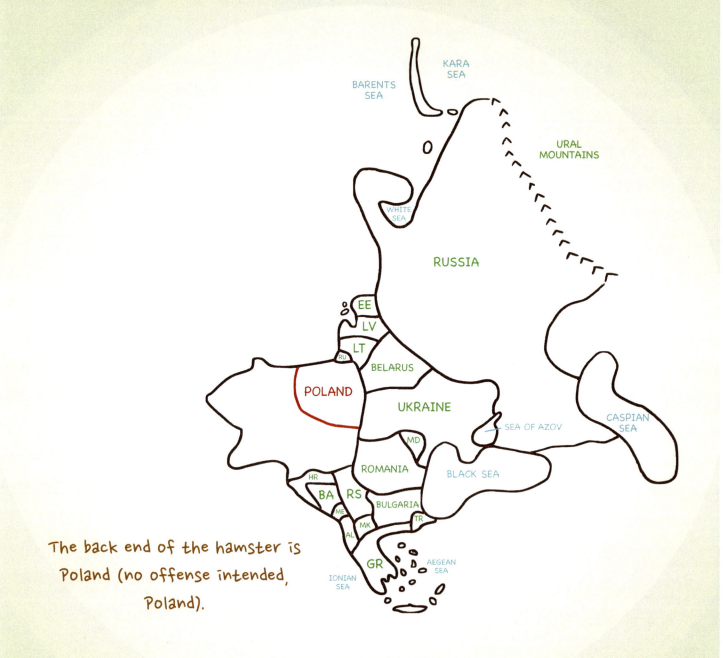

The back end of the hamster is Poland (no offense intended, Poland).

SLOVAKIA

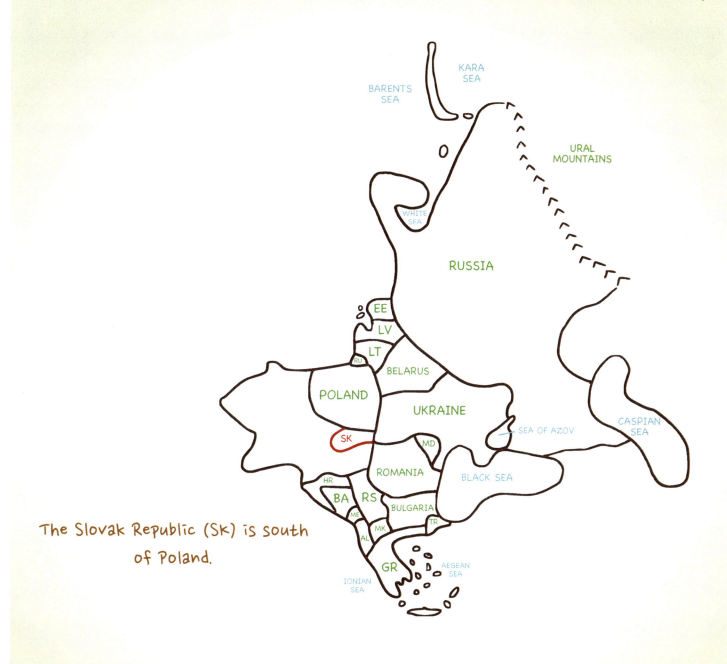

The Slovak Republic (SK) is south of Poland.

HUNGARY

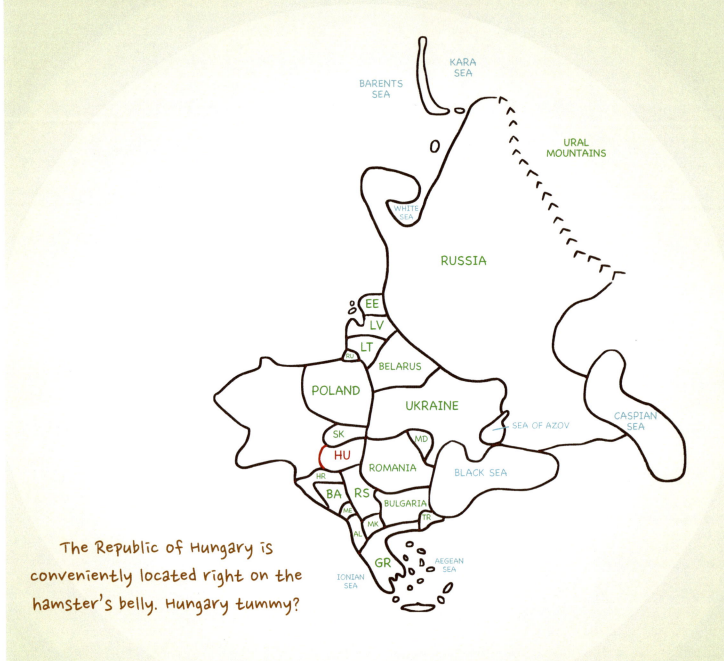

The Republic of Hungary is conveniently located right on the hamster's belly. Hungary tummy?

SLOVENIA

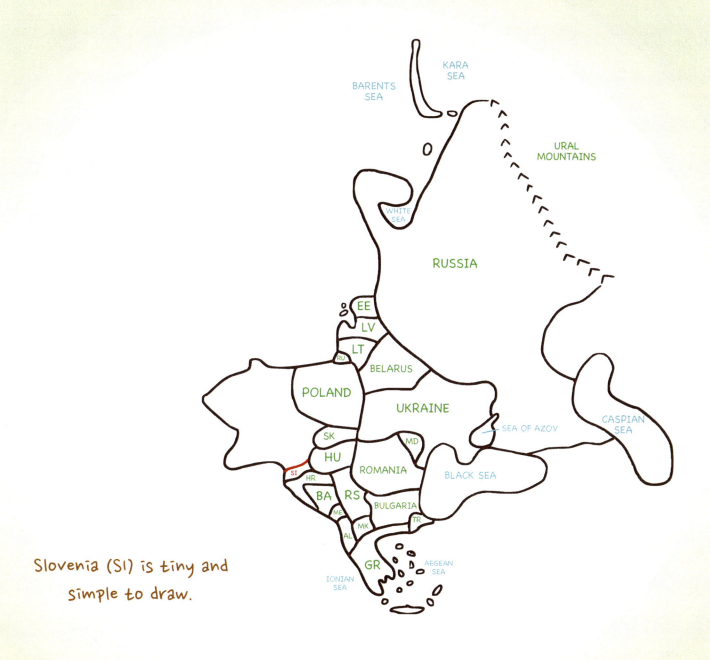

Slovenia (SI) is tiny and simple to draw.

CZECH REPUBLIC

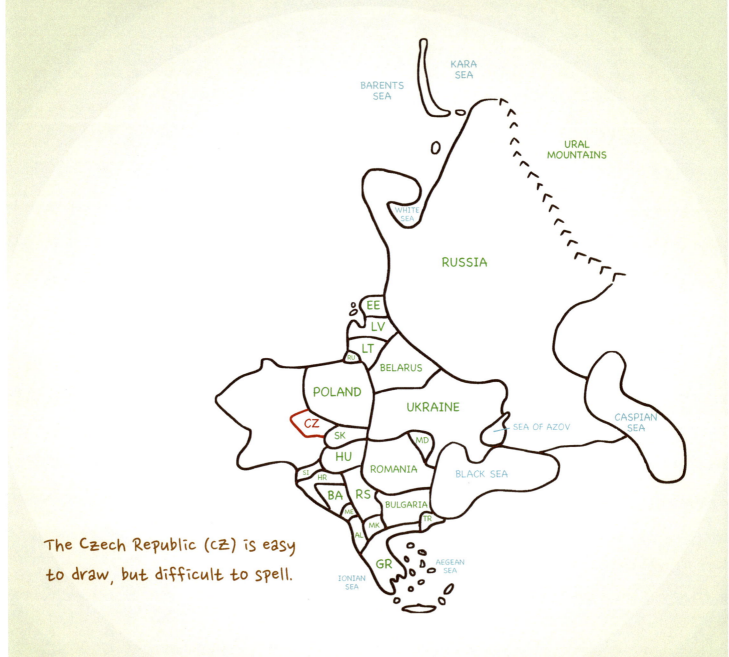

The Czech Republic (CZ) is easy to draw, but difficult to spell.

AUSTRIA

Austria (AT) is next.

LIECHTENSTEIN

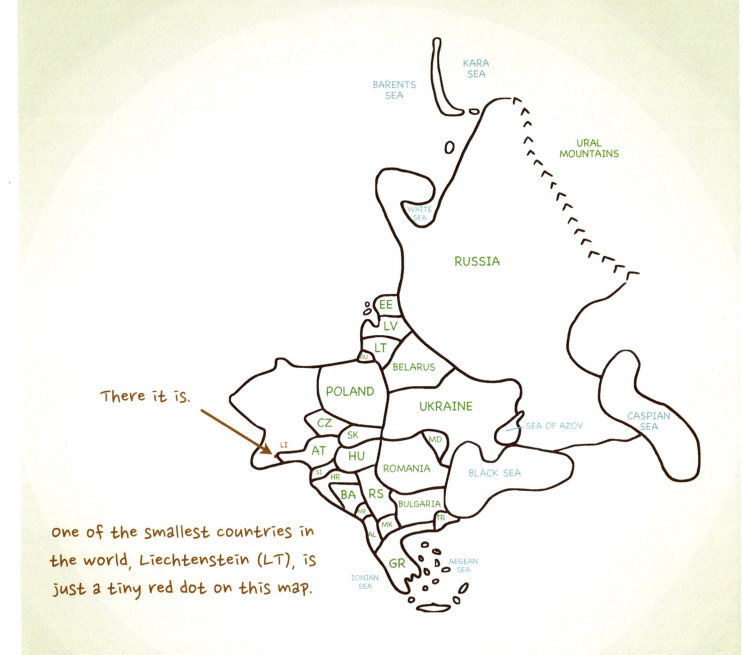

There it is.

One of the smallest countries in the world, Liechtenstein (LT), is just a tiny red dot on this map.

SWITZERLAND

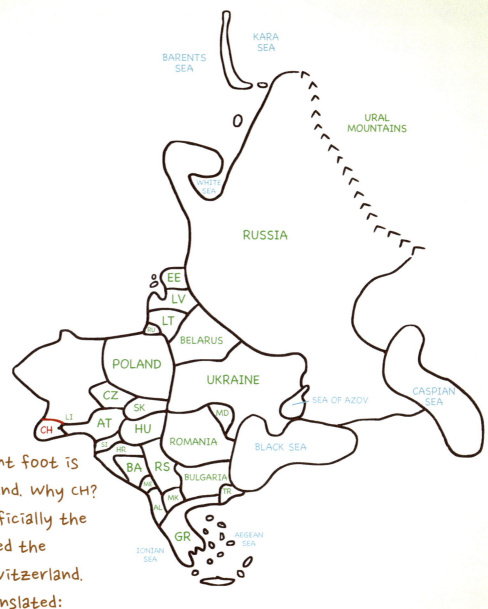

The hamster's front foot is stepping in Switzerland. Why CH? It's complicated. Officially the country is called the confederation of Switzerland. In Latin it is translated: "Confoederatio Helvetica" = CH. Whew!

GERMANY

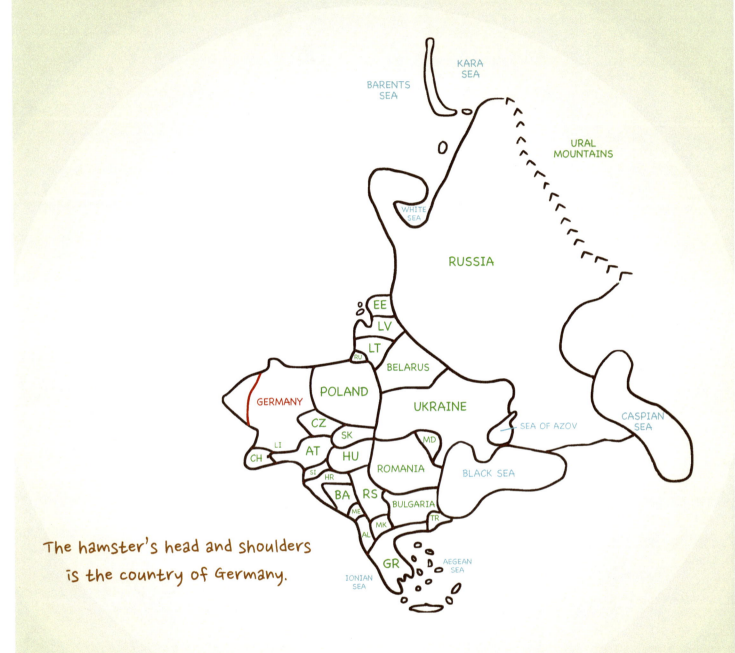

The hamster's head and shoulders is the country of Germany.

NETHERLANDS

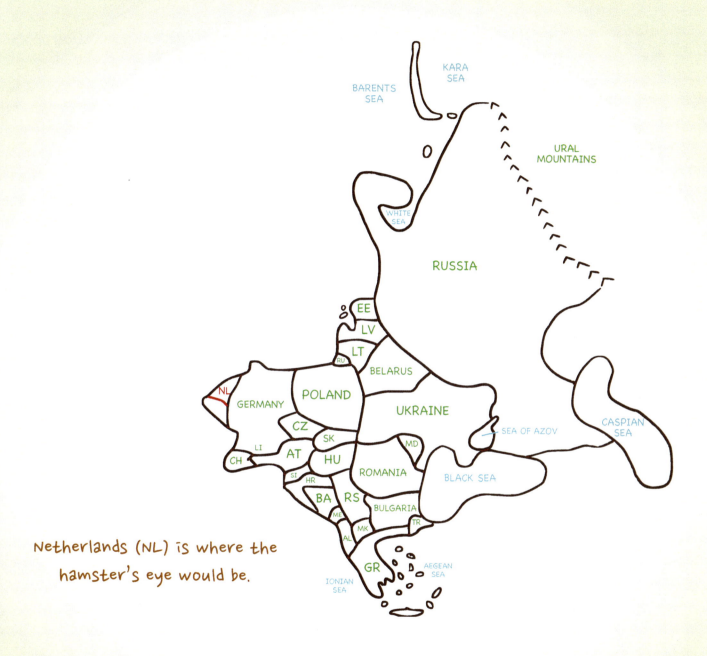

Netherlands (NL) is where the hamster's eye would be.

BELGIUM & LUXEMBOURG

Belgium (BE) is the hamster's nose, and Luxembourg (LU) is its tiny chin.

BALTIC BLOB & SEA

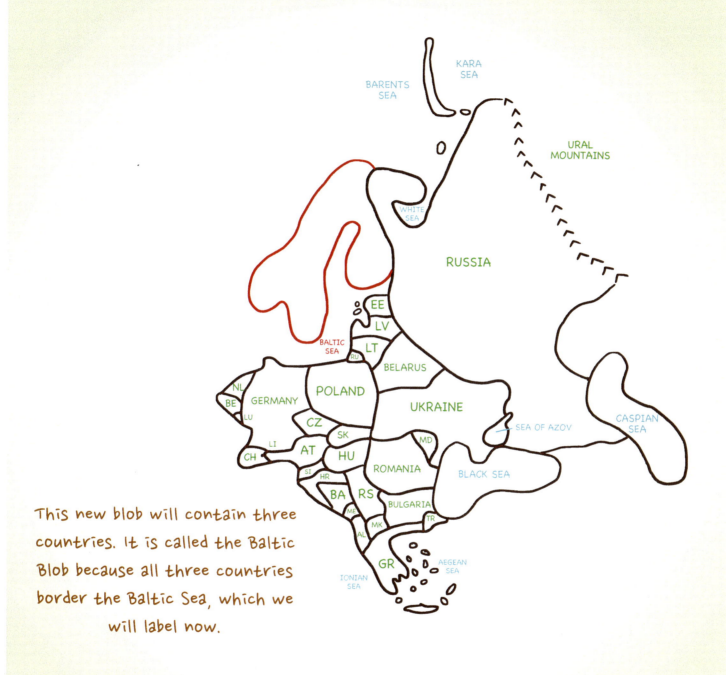

This new blob will contain three countries. It is called the Baltic Blob because all three countries border the Baltic Sea, which we will label now.

FINLAND

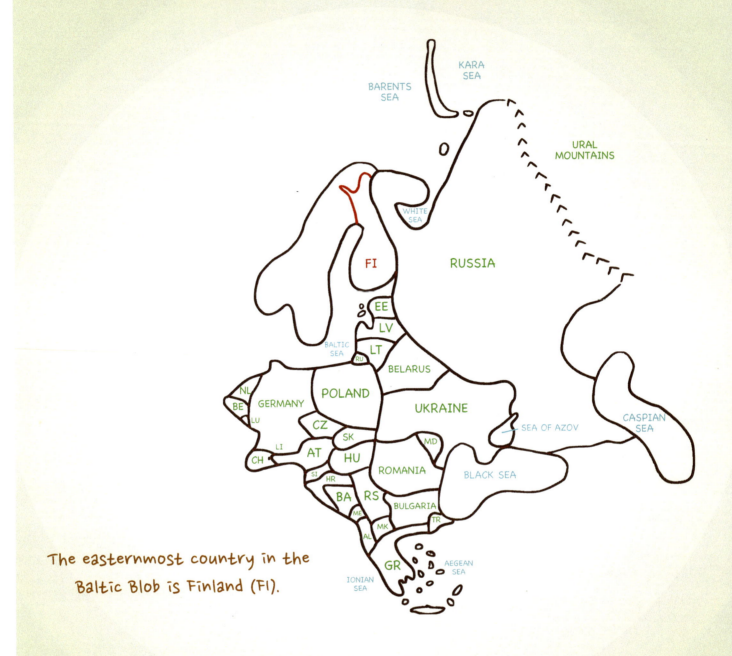

The easternmost country in the Baltic Blob is Finland (FI).

SWEDEN & NORWAY

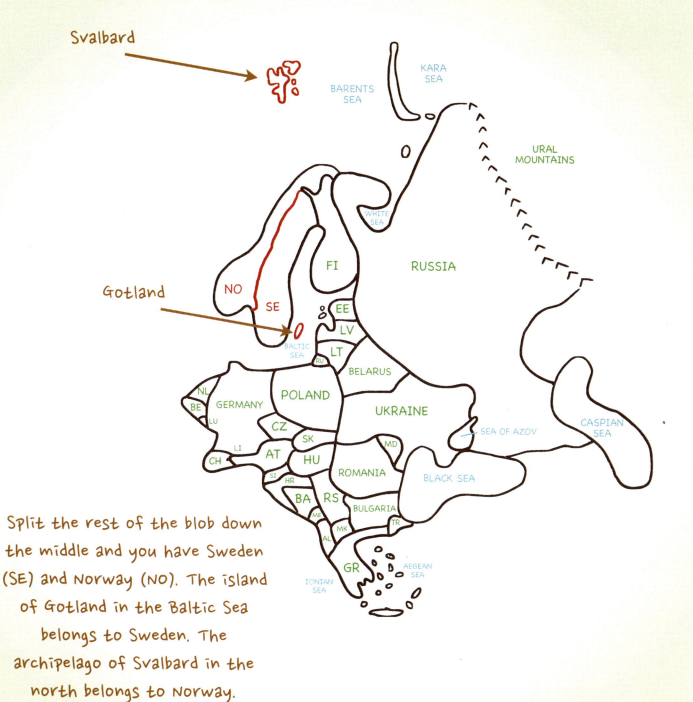

Svalbard

Gotland

Split the rest of the blob down the middle and you have Sweden (SE) and Norway (NO). The island of Gotland in the Baltic Sea belongs to Sweden. The archipelago of Svalbard in the north belongs to Norway.

NORWEGIAN SEA

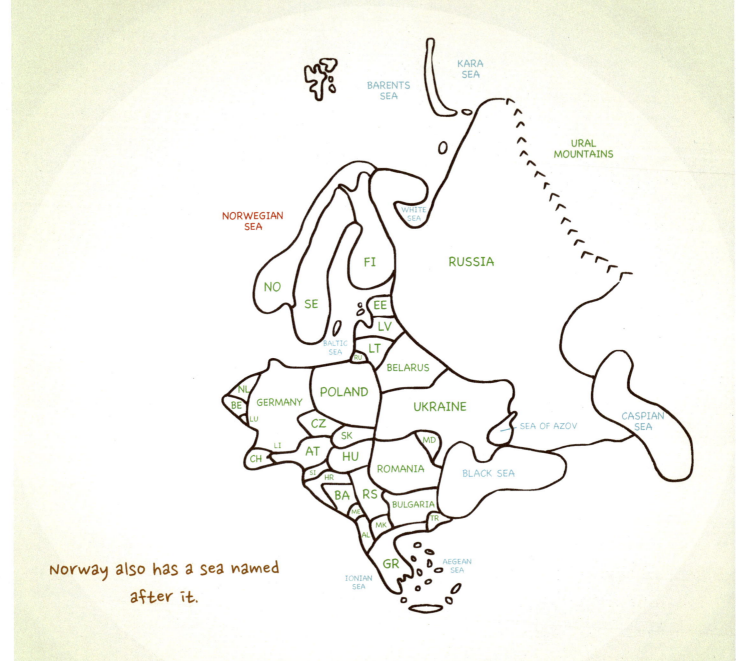

Norway also has a sea named after it.

DENMARK

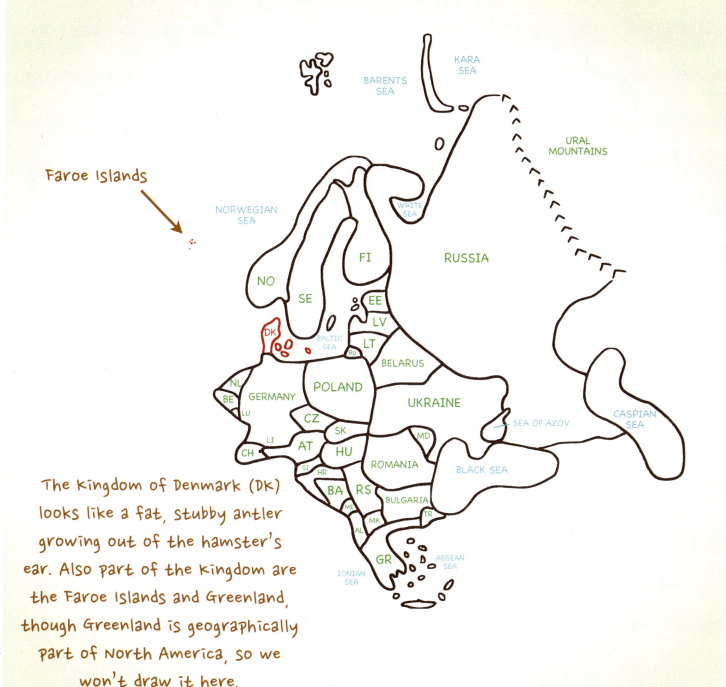

Faroe Islands

The Kingdom of Denmark (DK) looks like a fat, stubby antler growing out of the hamster's ear. Also part of the kingdom are the Faroe Islands and Greenland, though Greenland is geographically part of North America, so we won't draw it here.

ITALY

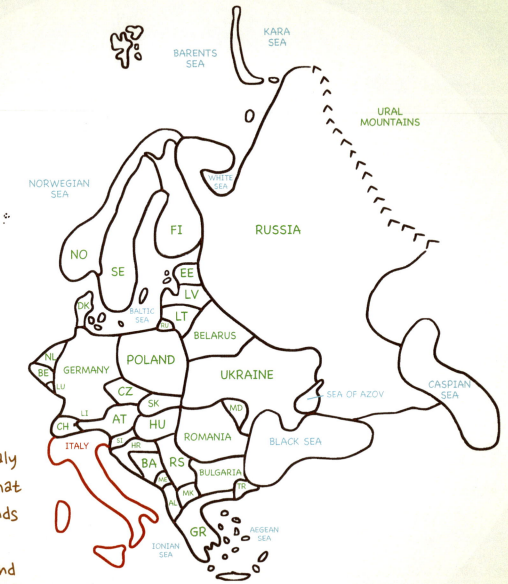

The country of Italy looks like a boot that is kicking the islands of Sicily (the southern island) and Sardinia (the northern island).

SAN MARINO & ADRIATIC SEA

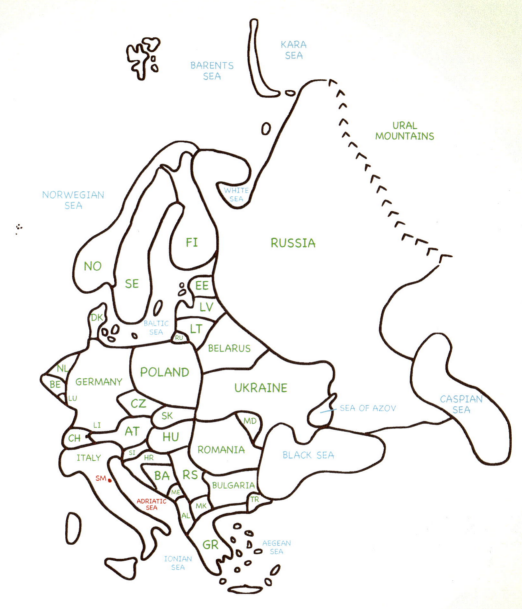

Another tiny independent country is San Marino (SM), and the body of water between Italy and eastern Europe is the Adriatic sea.

VATICAN CITY

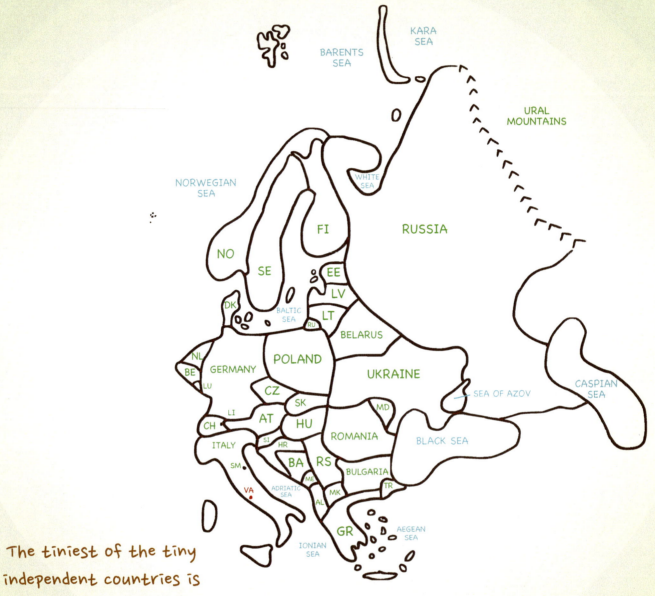

The tiniest of the tiny independent countries is Vatican City (VA). It is located on Italy's "knee."

FRANCE

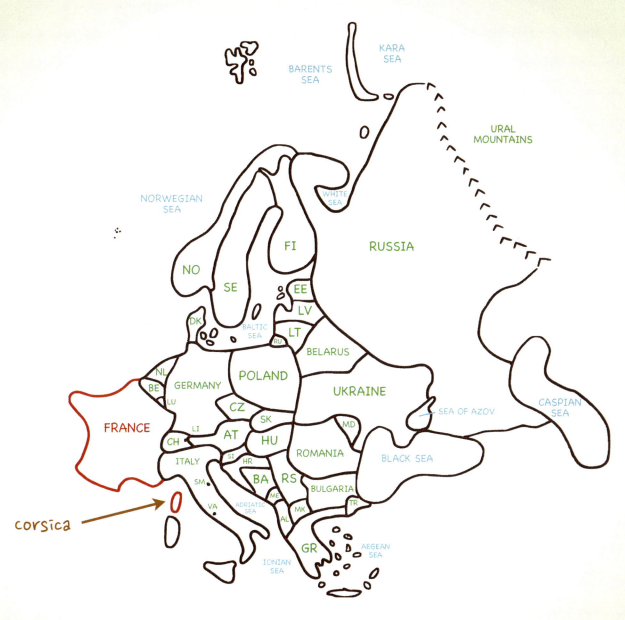

corsica

France has an indescribable shape (a rhinoceros head?). It also owns the island of Corsica and several other territories that are not in the continent of Europe.

MONACO

Monaco (MC) is another tiny independent country.

SPAIN

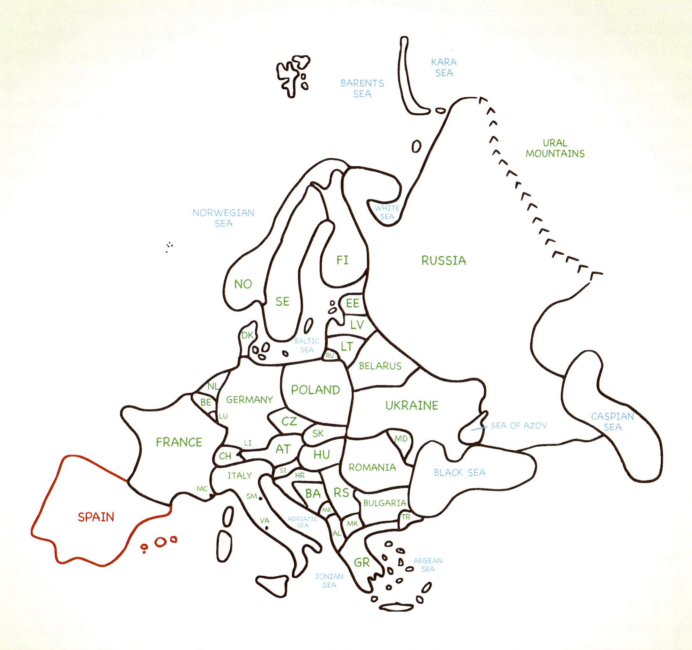

Spain is a large squarish country. The Balearic Islands, which belong to Spain, are are found near its eastern coast.

ANDORRA

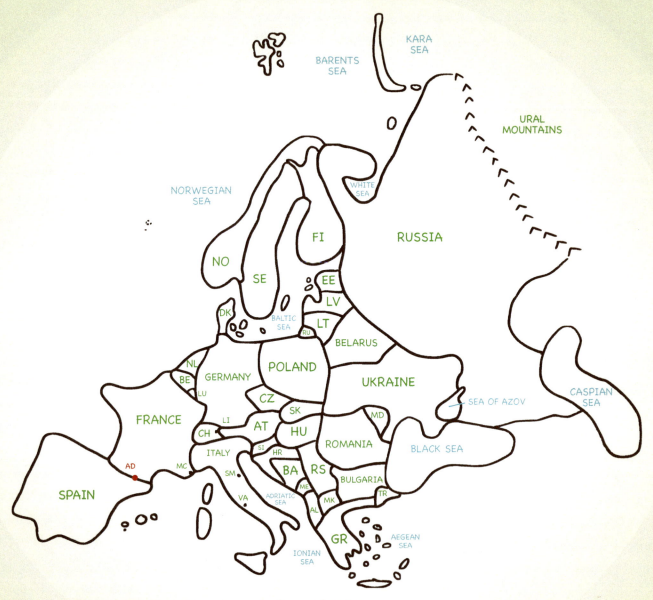

Andorra (AD) is yet another tiny independent country between France and Spain.

BAY OF BISCAY

The Bay of Biscay is a body of water between France and Spain.

STRAIT OF GIBRALTAR

The Strait of Gibraltar is a body of water between Spain and North Africa. Don't worry, we haven't forgotten about Portugal.

PORTUGAL

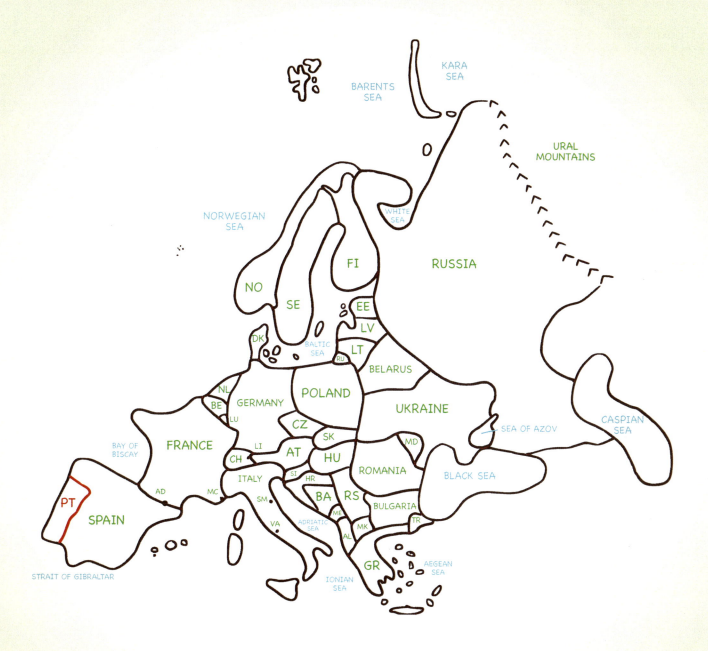

Portugal (PT) is a long rectangular country on the western edge of Spain.

MEDITERRANEAN SEA

The large body of water between Europe and North Africa is the Mediterranean Sea.

UNITED KINGDOM

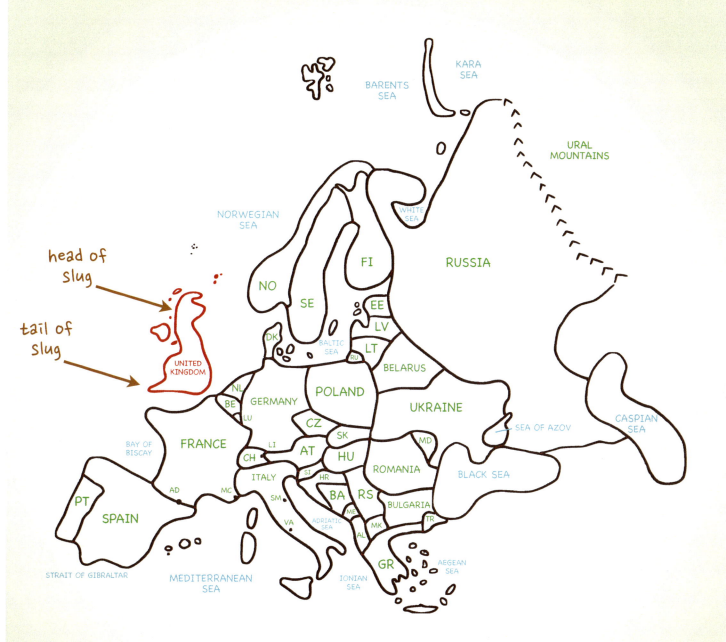

head of slug
tail of slug

The UK looks like a slug traveling eastward and has a collection of islands. The large island is Northern Ireland which is part of the UK.

IRELAND

The Republic of Ireland (IE) is independent of the UK and is attached to Northern Ireland.

NORTH SEA

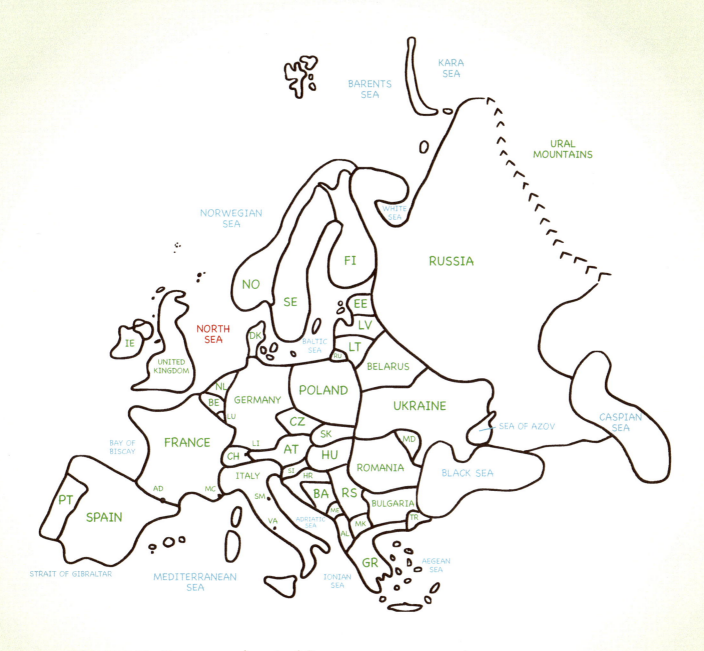

The North Sea is sandwiched between the UK and continental Europe.

ENGLISH CHANNEL

The English channel flows between the UK and France.

ICELAND

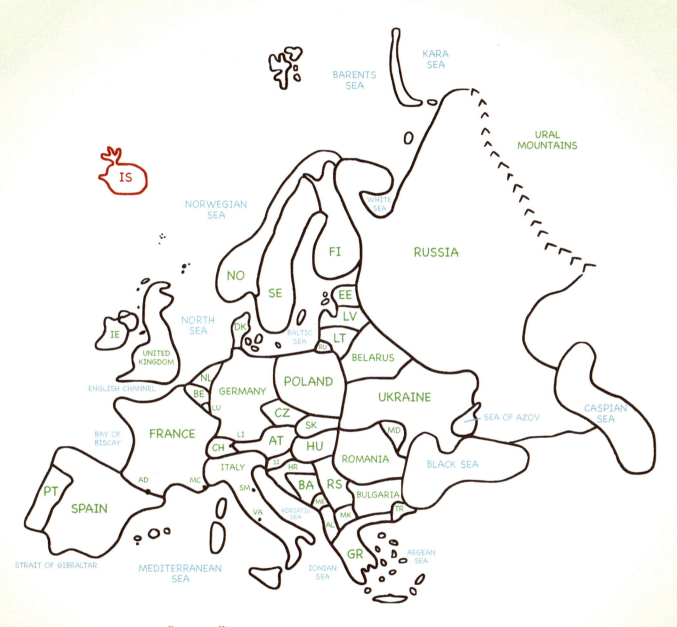

Iceland (IS), spelled "Ísland" in Icelandic, looks like a puffer fish with a three-pronged antler.

ARCTIC OCEAN

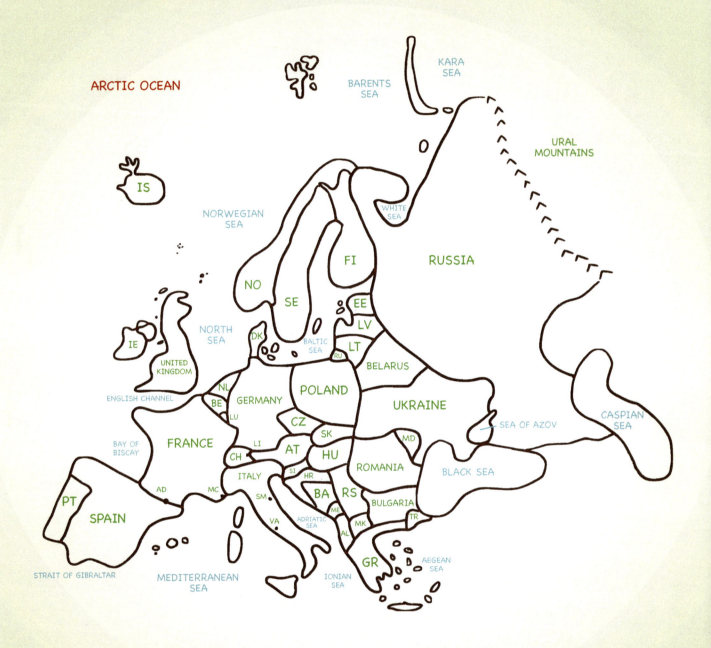

North of Europe is the Arctic Ocean.

Instructions

The Drawing

For this drawing use a plain 8 1/2 x 11 piece of paper turned horizontally. Follow the instructions in red, page by page, until the end of the book is reached, labeling the countries as you go. It is helpful for the student, when drawing each step, to ask "Where does the line begin?" and "Where does it end?" It is also helpful to mark these beginnings and endings with a dot before drawing the line.

The map can be drawn all at once, but students may find it easier to master smaller portions of the map at a time. After drawing five or six countries students may want to pause and practice what they have learned.

For younger students I recommend using ledger-sized (11x17) paper for drawing the maps. This size allows students with less-refined motor skills to draw larger without worrying about running off the end of the page. This size of paper can still be folded in half and stored in a 8 1/2 x 11 binder.

Coloring

If the student wishes to color the map, I recommend first inking it with a thin, black, permanent marker. This will help maintain the integrity of the outline and give the final product a more "professional" look.

Enjoy.

For Lillian with love,

URAL MOUNTAINS

edge of paper

Leave some room here . . .

URAL MOUNTAINS

and here.

Turn your paper sideways so that it is wider than it is tall. In the upper right corner draw the Ural Mountains.

The part of Russia that is west of the Urals is in Europe and the part that is east is in Asia.

ATLANTIC OCEAN

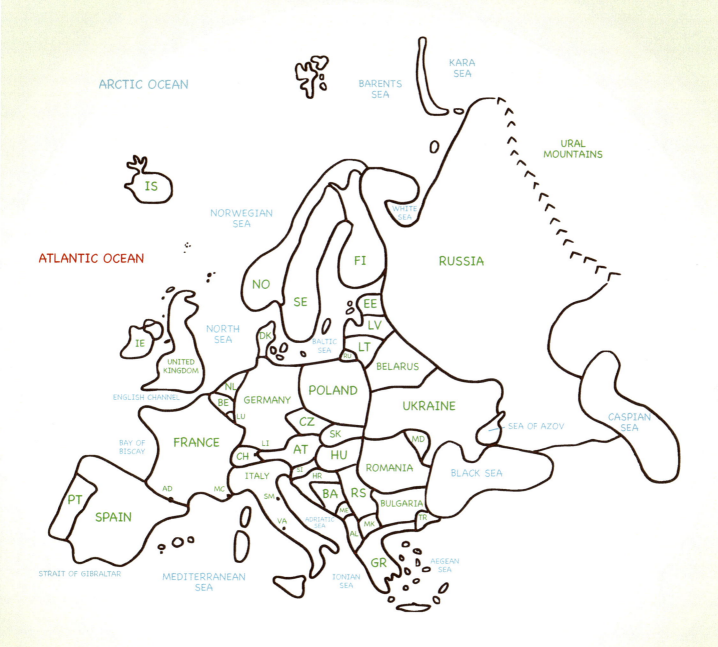

And finally, west of Europe is the Atlantic Ocean.

EUROPE

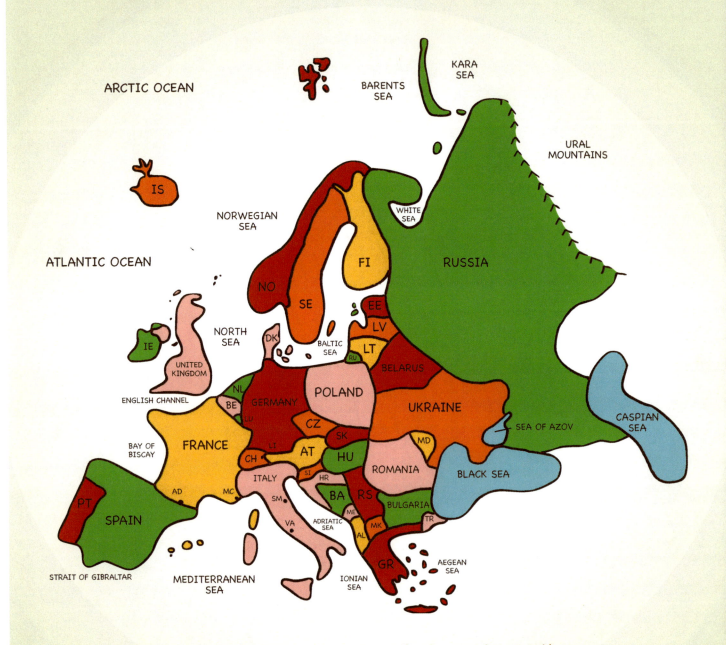

Ink and color your map, and you are finished!
Well done! Brilliant! Good show!

Made in the USA
Las Vegas, NV
02 February 2021